AMERICA'S REAL FIRST

Thanksgiving

This is a gift from the:

Danville Library Foundation

AMERICA'S REAL FIRST WITHDRAWN
Thanksgiving

St. Augustine, Florida, September 8, 1565

Robyn Gioia

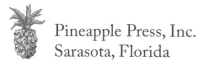

Pineapple Press, Inc.
Sarasota, Florida

Illustration Credits

Pages 1, 5, 33, 34, and 39: copyright © 2007 Cox-Deaton; Robert Deaton, Historical artist for the Florida Museum of History, Tallahassee, FL COX♥DEATON

Pages 2 (left) and 26 (bottom): Florida State Archives.

Pages 2 (right) and 21 (top): Courtesy of Theodore Morris, www.floridalosttribes.com

Pages 2 and 36 (top right): Courtesy of Charles S. Boning.

Pages 3, 28, 29, 31, and 35: Courtesy of Frank Suddeth.

Page 7: Benedict Arias Montanus Sacrae Geographiae Tabula Ex Antiquissimourm Published 1569-72. Courtesy of Harry S. Newman, Old Print Shop, New York, N.Y.

Page 9: Ortelius, Abraham. La Florida. From the Additamentum to the Theatrum Orbis Terarrum, 1584. Courtesy of the P.K. Yonge Library of Florida History, University of Florida Libraries.

Page 10: From History of the Reign of Philip the Second King of Spain by William H. Prescott. Vol. 1. Philadelphia: J. B. Lippincott & Co., 1880.

Page 11 (all photos): Courtesy of David White.

Page 12 (left): The J. Paul Getty museum, Los Angeles; Artist: Unknown; Title: The Lamb Defeating the Ten Kings; About 1220–1235; Tempera colors and gold leaf on parchment, 11 9/16 x 9 ¼ in.

Page 12 (right): Courtesy of David White

Page 13 (top): The J. Paul Getty museum, Los Angeles; Artist Circle of Fernando Gallego; Title: Pieta; About 1490–1500, oil on canvas, 22 1/8 x 16x2 in.

Page 13: Drawing: Joris Hoefnagel, 1566. Courtesy of Historic Cities Research Project http://historic-cities.huji.ac.il The Hebrew University of Jerusalem

Page 14 (left): The J. Paul Getty Museum, Los Angeles; Artist: Unknown; Title: Hispano-Moresque Basin; Spain, Mid-15th century; Media: Tin-glazed and luster-painted earthenware; Size: Diameter 49.5 cm

Page 14 (top right): The J. Paul Getty Museum Villa Collection, Malibu, CA; Artist Unknown; Title: Winged Feline; Spain, 700–575 B.C.; Media: Bronze; Size: 61 x W: 19.4 x D: 33 cm

Page 14 (bottom right): The J. Paul Getty Museum, Los Angeles; Artist: Unknown; Title: Tile Floor; Spain, about 1425-1450; Size: 121.92 x 182.88 cm

Page 15: The J. Paul Getty Museum, Los Angeles; Artist: Michael Lupi de Çandiu (Illuminator); Title: Initial E: An Equestrian Duel Between a Creditor and a Debtor; Spain, about 1290–1310; Media: Tempera colors, gold leaf, ink on parchment; Size: Leaf: 36.5 x 24 cm

Page 16: Hurricanes: NASA. Image produced by Hal Pierce, Laboratory for Atmospheres, NASA Goddard Space Flight Center.

Pages 17, 20, 21 (bottom), 22, 23, 24, and 25 (bottom): Jacques Le Moyne. Courtesy of Pelotes Island Nature Preserve.

Page 18: Courtesy of Pelotes Island Nature Preserve.

Page 19 (both photos): Courtesy of Doug Alderson.

Page 25 (all photos): Courtesy of the Florida Museum of Natural History. Photos by Jeff Gage.

Page 26 (bottom): Courtesy of Jean Moran.

Pages 27 and 43: Courtesy of Robyn Gioia.

Page 30: Courtesy of Pelotes Island Nature Preserve.

Page 37 (top): David Meek for the Florida Humanities Council.

Page 37 (bottom): Courtesy of Ray Ashton.

Page 40, 41 (top left and bottom left), and 42 (both): St. Augustine, Ponte Vedra & The Beaches Visitors and Convention Bureau.

Page 41 (both left): Courtesy of the state of Florida.

Copyright © 2007, 2014 by Robyn Gioia

Inquiries should be addressed to:
Pineapple Press, Inc.
P.O. Box 3889
Sarasota, Florida 34230
www.pineapplepress.com

Library of Congress Cataloging-in-Publication Data
Gioia, Robyn.
America's real first Thanksgiving : St. Augustine, Florida, September 8, 1565 / Robyn Gioia. -- 1st ed.
    p. cm.
Includes bibliographical references and index.
ISBN 978-1-56164-712-5 (paperback : alk. paper)
1. Saint Augustine (Fla.)--History--16th century. 2. Saint Augustine (Fla.)--History--16th century--Pictorial works. 3. Thanksgiving Day--Florida--Saint Augustine--History--16th century. 4. Spaniards--Florida--Saint Augustine--History--16th century. 5. Timucua Indians--Florida--Saint Augustine--History--16th century. 6. Saint Augustine (Fla.)--Social life and customs--16th century. 7. Saint Augustine (Fla.)--Ethnic relations--History--16th century. 8. Florida--History--To 1821. I. Title.
F319.S2L47 2006
975.9'1801--dc22
                                                                                2006037281

First Edition
10 9 8 7 6 5 4 3 2 1

Design: Doris Halle
Printed in USA

Contents

1. The World in 1565

Long ago many people thought the world was flat, but educated people began to consider the idea that the Earth is a sphere. In the Age of Exploration, from the late 15th century to the early 17th century, ships set out from Europe to find out what might be on the other side of this sphere. They were anxious to explore new lands and claim their resources, particularly gold.

One of the countries sending out explorers was Spain. The first explorer Spain sent, an Italian named Chistopher Columbus, landed on an island in the New World in 1492. He finally made it to the mainland in 1498. Then many other explorers ventured forth, including Juan Ponce de León, who landed in a place he named La Florida when he first landed there in 1513. In 1565 Pedro Menéndez de Avilés came to La Florida to establish a settlement.

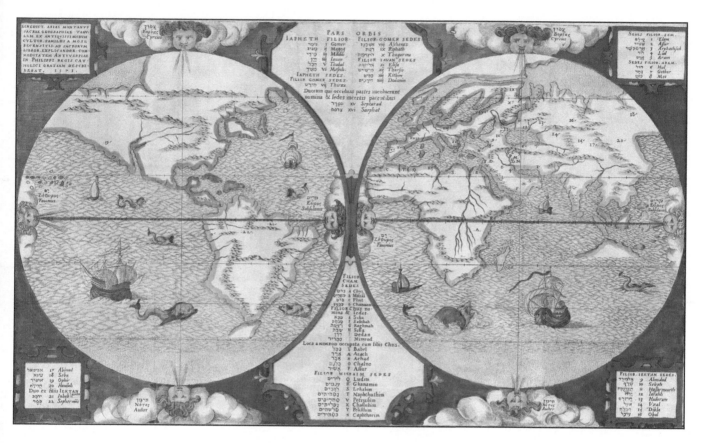

This important map appeared in the Plantin Polyglot Bible in 1569–72. It was prepared under the patronage of King Philip II of Spain. Look closely at the shapes of the continents. How are they different today? Notice the size of the Florida peninsula and its relationship to Texas and California. Note the ships and sea creatures swimming in the oceans and the great gusts of winds influencing the weather.

2. Uncharted Lands

When the explorers arrived in the New World, they had at first, of course, no maps to guide them. Each expedition recorded what they found, and gradually the shape of the North and South American continents took form on maps.

The New World that the European explorers found at first appeared wild and uninhabited, but soon they learned that people lived there. Today we know that millions of native inhabitants had lived in these lands for thousands of years before the arrival of the Europeans. There were many different tribes of native people, each with a distinct culture—their own patterns of knowledge, beliefs, and ways of surviving in their environment. These cultures were very different from the European cultures that the explorers knew.

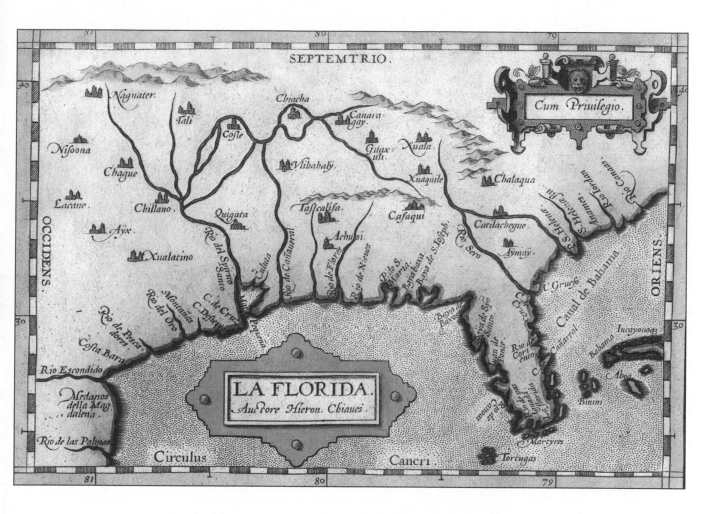

1584 map of Florida. Notice the shape of the coastline and the islands to the east.

3. Spain in the 1560s

Spain was a thriving Renaissance country in Europe in the late 16th century. After the Middle Ages, European countries put a new emphasis on knowledge, the arts, exploration, politics, and commerce. By the 1560s Spain was an important European power ruled by King Philip II.

Philip II was crowned king in 1556. During his reign, Spain became the world leader in global exploration, though Philip himself stayed in El Escorial, his palace outside Madrid. He ruled until his death in 1598.

Bottom: The exterior of the Escorial Palace near Madrid, built by King Philip II between 1562 and 1584. Right: A magnificent painted ceiling in the Escorial Palace. Below: Detail of ceiling.

The Roman Catholic Church and its rituals were a large part of people's daily lives. Most art of the times displayed religious scenes. Crosses could be seen everywhere. They adorned homes, public buildings, and churches. Religious groups such as the Jesuits and the Franciscans served as missionaries and traveled to faraway lands to teach others about the Roman Catholic faith.

The Lamb of God defeats each king as they approach in this early Spanish religious painting.

San Pablo Church, Valladolid, Spain. Notice the detailed architecture of the 16th century. The Roman Catholic Church had great influence over society.

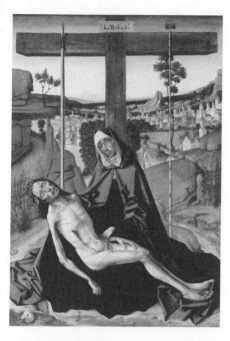

The Virgin Mary grieves over the death of her son in this Spanish painting.

Toledo, Spain. Since it is situated in the middle of Spain, among mountainous terrain and untouched lands, access to the town was extremely difficult, thus protecting the town from enemy attack. The houses were large and the interiors more beautiful than the exteriors. The city had many churches known for their beauty, numerous monasteries and convents, hospitals, a house for what they called "the weak-minded and the insane," and 17 markets full of supplies. It was known for its weavers of silk and wool, as well as clergy, liberal arts, and handicrafts.

The wealthiest people depended on others to do the manual work. Much of the labor came from enslaved Africans. Owning slaves wouldn't be outlawed until much later, in the 1800s. Spain had universities, grand architecture, and theaters where the people could watch the latest plays.

The marketplaces were full of goods. Skilled doctors treated the sick, judges represented the law, merchants traveled the seas, and administrators organized the empire.

Below: Painted dishes like this may have been used for serving or as a decoration.
Right: This winged feline was probably created in Spain as early as 1000 A.D.
Lower right: Spanish tiles of the era were elaborately decorated.

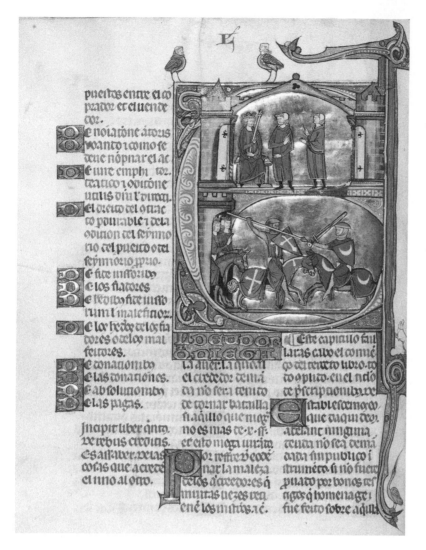

Part of a medieval book, illustrated with ink, colored paint, and gold leaf. In the top panel the king listens to a dispute between a creditor and debtor. The battle in the panel below may demonstrate what would happen if there were no legal system to prevent bloodshed.

The laws that governed the country provided stability but would seem very harsh compared to today's standards. The king's word was absolute law, and it was the time of the Spanish Inquisition. This was a very brutal period in history when the church and government told society what religious beliefs to follow. It was not uncommon for a person to be put to death if he or she did not obey.

The country had a well-established military. In many respects, their society was modern and sophisticated.

4. Florida in the 1560s

Life in sunny Florida was very different from life in Spain. Florida was not a modern country. There were no grand churches with high ceilings or bustling marketplaces. There were no castles or imposing naval fleets. Universities did not exist. Great scientists of the day did not meet to discuss the laws of nature or how things worked. The landscape was as it had been for a thousand years, much of it swampy. The sun was intense and the air hot and humid. There were clouds of mosquitoes and big alligators. Birds were everywhere in large flocks that could almost fill the sky. The weather from the sea could be dangerous. Hurricanes could cause large waves and incredible gusts of winds.

Hurricanes are not new in Florida. The native peoples, many of whom lived along the coasts, had no radar and TV weatherman to tell them a hurricane was coming.

Look closely at this map of Florida, which had been previously
uncharted. The French artist Jacques Le Moyne inserted some
geographical names and positions of rivers and places as he heard
about them from the Indians. Look at the middle of the map
along the top border. That wiggly line represents a border between
land and water, showing how the artist was unfamiliar with
the terrain.

Along Florida's coasts, the native people ate shellfish. It was nutritious, plentiful, and easy to harvest. The shells accumulated into tall mounds like this one. When the Spanish arrived, they no doubt saw mounds like this all along the coast as they were searching for a good place to land. They were soon to meet the people who made them, the Timucua. The Timucua are sometimes called the People of the Shell Mounds.

Much of Florida looked like this in the 1560s. Much of the low-lying Florida peninsula is wetland. Swamps are forested wetlands. Mosquitoes, snakes, and alligators are a natural part of wetland ecology. The Timucua had developed ways of living in this environment. They moved easily through the forests and swamps.

Alligators were plentiful in early Florida. The Timucua had learned how to hunt and kill them for food. The drawing by a European artist on page 22 shows that the natives hunted them using a long pole. But parts of the drawing are untrue. Alligators are not nearly as big as shown. Most alligators are no longer than 15 feet.

5. The Timucua, St. Augustine's Native Americans

When the Spanish arrived, a community of Native Americans called the Timucua lived throughout northeast Florida. There were at least thirty Timucuan towns and villages, and one of them, the village of Seloy, was on the North River near where St. Augustine would be founded. The circular houses, covered with thatched palm leaves, were arranged along the bay. The communities were organized into chiefdoms with one person in charge, a great chief called *cacique* by the Spaniards and *holato* by the Timucua.

A Timucuan village. The chief's dwelling would have been positioned in the middle of town and partly buried to escape the intense Florida sun.

This painting shows what Chief Outina of the Timucuas might have looked like. He is painted red and decorated in tattoos displayed by nobility. As was the tradition, his hair is worn at the top of his head in a knot. His long fingernails have been sharpened against a shell until pointed, and his ears decorated with small inflated fish bladders placed through pierced lobes. Raccoon tails, eagle feathers, turkey vulture feathers, copper breast plate, shell beads, deer hide robe, chert (stone) spear points, and painted hide straps are also part of his outerwear.

The chief and his nobles customarily met on certain days to discuss matters of importance. The chief asked his priest and elders, one at a time, to deliver their opinions. The women prepared casina, a drink for those on the council who were proven to be brave warriors.

Hoes made from fish bones were used for preparing the land for planting.

Opposite: Great care was taken in the smoking and drying of meats so they wouldn't spoil. Meats prepared in this fashion were well preserved and could be stored for later.

The Timucua caught an alligator by shoving a pole down its opened mouth. Then they flipped the alligator over on its back to expose the softer underbelly, where they pierced the skin with clubs and arrows. Notice the exaggeration of the alligator's features. It is believed that the artist was not familiar with the features of a real alligator. (See page 30 for more about Jacques Le Moyne, the artist who drew these images of the Timucua.)

The land and sea had provided the Timucua with an endless source of food for thousands of years. They hunted, fished, and farmed. They hunted white-tailed deer, alligator, and wild turkey. They were very clever at catching fish—sometimes by netting them, sometimes by using spears, and sometimes by trapping them in weirs (or fish corrals). The women planted crops of corn, beans, and squash by poking holes in the soil, dropping the seeds in, and covering them over.

The Timucua selected large deerskins to wear over their heads, so they could see out the eyes holes like a mask, giving them an advantage in the hunt.

Fruits were gathered twice a year and carried home in canoes to be stored in granaries built of stones and earth. Positioned away from the sun's rays, the granaries were used for a variety of provisions needing to be preserved.

Because of the hot and humid weather, the people wore little in the way of clothing. The men wore loincloths made of deerskins. Although the women sometimes wore deerskins, they mostly wore coverings of woven Spanish moss. The men and women of the noble class were decorated with colorful skin designs of red, black, and azure (a light shade of blue). These designs could have been tattoos, but historical illustrations show some individuals having different designs in different pictures. It is possible these designs could have been drawn using body paint, but it seems more likely they used a combination of tattoos and paint.

Far left: These Timucua ornaments and tools are made from local chert and coral.

Top right: The Timucua made many of their tools and weapons from shells.

Left: Timucua made pins and beads from shell, stone, and bone.

Look closely at the figures below and you'll notice the tattoo patterns on the king and queen. It was the fashion to paint the mouth blue. The king was clad in a deerskin painted with many colors and followed by two men carrying fans. The queen and her maidens were clothed in Spanish moss woven into slender threads of bluish-green.

6. The Founding of St. Augustine, 1565

In 1565, Spanish Admiral Pedro Menéndez de Avilés crossed the Atlantic Ocean and traveled along the coast of Florida, near where Juan Ponce de León had discovered this land 52 years earlier in 1513. He was looking for a place to land his ships. King Philip II had sent the admiral to protect Spain's claim on southeast North America. Jean Ribault, a French explorer, had also entered the area to set up a new colony and claim the area for France. France wanted to control the new land and keep out the Spanish settlers.

Pedro Menéndez de Avilés

Birthplace of Pedro Menéndez in Avilés, Spain. He was born there February 15, 1519.

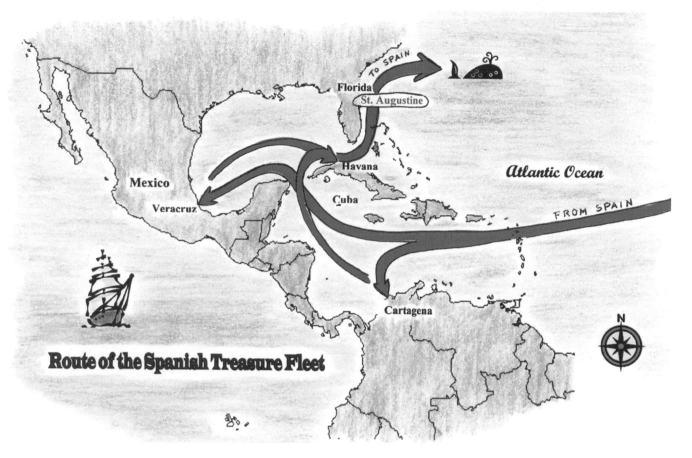

Spanish Florida 1565–1763. Route of the Spanish Treasure Fleet.

The sea-lanes, routes used by ships for trading, needed Admiral Menéndez's protection too. The Gulf Stream runs northward from the Gulf of Mexico, through the Straits of Florida, and into the Atlantic Ocean along Florida's Atlantic coast. It was an important water route used by the treasure fleets or *flotas*. A fleet was comprised of 30 to 90 Spanish ships used for carrying European goods to the Spanish colonies in the Americas. On the return trip, the fleet would transport colonial products such as gold and silver back to Spain.

Spanish Galleon

These large ships were first built in the 15th and 16th centuries. Their main use was as warships. Spain also used them to cross the Atlantic to explore the New World. They were made from oak, a strong, hard wood, and weighed as much as two jumbo jets!

Menéndez was searching for a place along the coast that could offer shelter for his vessels. He needed to be near a river for traveling inland. The position of the land needed to protect them from the enemy, yet be close enough to allow them to attack the French foothold at Fort Caroline. During his search, Menéndez discovered a shallow sandbar across an inlet 30 miles south of the French fort. The sandbar ensured that larger ships couldn't pass into the harbor except on the flood tide. That would make the harbor safer from the large French ships. This was the site he needed. He named this place after Saint Augustine of Hippo, on whose feast day he had spotted Florida's shore.

Menéndez sailed along the north Florida coast searching for shelter.

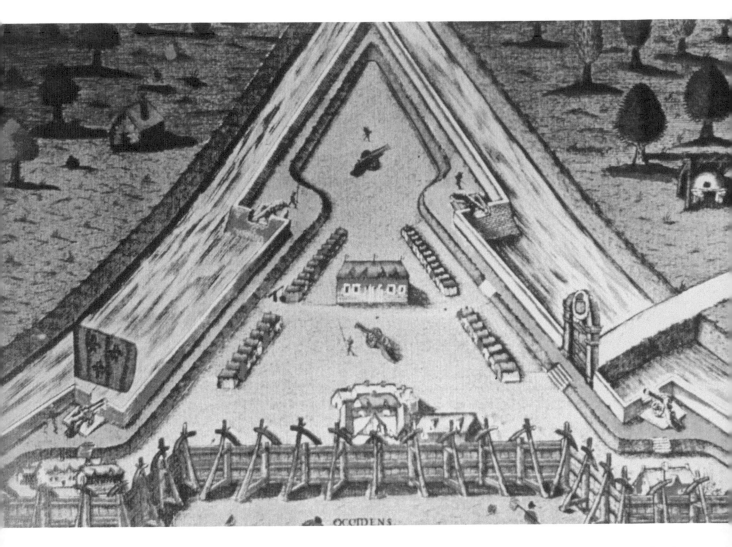

OCCIDENS.

Fort Caroline was located 30 miles north of St. Augustine. It was built in 1564 by the French explorer René de Laudonnière. Fortunately Laudonnière brought with him an artist, Jacques Le Moyne, who recorded what he saw in this new land: the place and especially the people. The French fort and most of the French people there did not survive, but Jacques Le Moyne did survive and went back to France. An engraver named Theodore De Bry made engravings of Le Moyne's drawings. In 1591, De Bry published a book with the engravings and Le Moyne's description of his trip to Florida. For the first time, Europeans could see what life was like in America without sailing across the Atlantic Ocean.

Aboard Menéndez's galleon as one of his men sights land.

7. Day of Thanksgiving
September 8, 1565

Spain was a country of ceremony. As would be expected, Pedro Menéndez's landing was one of ritual. There was a proper way of doing things and landing on foreign soil. This meant Menéndez would follow special procedures. With the Timucua watching on shore, Admiral Menéndez stepped formally from his launch. The air was filled with the sound of trumpets and the thundering of artillery. Dressed in full uniform and holding his head high, the admiral took his place on the newly claimed soil.

He was greeted by a chaplain carrying a cross and singing *Te Deum Laudamus,* a hymn of joy and thanksgiving. Father Francisco López de Mendoza Grajales had arrived earlier so he could welcome the admiral.

*Menéndez is rowed ashore and greeted with
great cermony at the future site of St. Augustine.*

A Mass of Thanksgiving for safe arrival in a new land.

As expected, the Spaniards knelt to kiss the cross. When the Timucua saw the honor being paid to the cross by the newcomers, they followed in reverence. They observed and imitated what was going on.

After that, a special Mass of Thanksgiving was given in the name of the Nativity of Our Lady to God for a safe journey and a new land. With a notary by his side, Menéndez claimed Florida for the Spanish Crown and was declared governor of the new land.

Timucua prepare wild turkey and grind corn in preparation for the feast.

Muscadine grapes are native to Florida and were part of the early Floridians' diet.

Then Menéndez provided a Thanksgiving feast for the Spanish, with the Timucua as guests. What kind of meal was it? The records don't really tell us, but we can suppose from the foods recorded in the ship's logs. The Spanish ate *cocido*, a rich stew made with pork, garbanzo beans, and onions. Hard sea biscuits and red wine would have been served with the stew.

Perhaps the Timucua provided meats such as wild turkey or venison. Or perhaps it was something exotic from the region, such as alligator, seafood, or tortoise—a dish described earlier by Father Francisco as tasting like veal. What did the native people eat? We know from what archaeologists have found that the Timucua ate deer, gopher tortoise, and fish like shark, mullet, and sea catfish. For vegetables they ate maize (corn), beans, and squash, along with nuts, fruit, and green leaves that they could gather.

Maize (corn) was an important basic food for the Florida natives. The different Florida tribes had different names for it, but they all translated as "our life."

Pork was a widely used meat in Spain, and Spanish explorers brought pigs with them to La Florida. Escaped pigs became wild and spread throughout the region. The native Floridians soon learned to hunt and eat them.

The gopher tortoise lives in sandy areas in the southeastern United States, including Florida's coasts. They dig long burrows in the sand. The Timucua undoubtedly ate them as part of their diet. Their burrows are home for many other creatures, like frogs and snakes, which were likely also eaten by the native people.

If we close our eyes, we can imagine the smell of a roaring fire. We can envision the Timucua savoring their first taste of onion and herbs in cocido, as well as the flavor of salted pork cooked into the stew. The Spaniards may be experiencing their first taste of alligator or bread made with corn. We can smell the fruity aroma of red wine in the cups and imagine the careful passing of food platters. While listening to the sounds of the day, we can hear the rapid beat of the Spanish tongue and the now-extinct language of the Timucua. And at dusk, we feel a gentle breeze roll in from the ocean while an enormous Florida sun slips suddenly below the tree-lined horizon, turning the sky around us brilliant shades of red and yellow.

Sharing of the Thanksgiving meal. The Spanish and the native people each offered their own specialties.

8. St. Augustine Today

Many centuries have passed and it is now the twenty-first century. Times have changed and Florida is no longer a land filled with Native Americans. In fact, the time of the Timucua has passed. Only history and archaeology can tell us about their presence in Florida and the impact they once had on events. And the time of the Spanish explorers has also come to a close, but their influence lives on through St. Augustine's historical architecture and records left behind.

Aviles Street, named after Avilés, Spain, hometown of Pedro Menéndez.

Castillo de San Marcos, a fort built by the Spanish between 1672 and 1695.

Flagler College. Spanish influence is evident throughout America's Ancient City today.

The Spanish Cross of Burgundy flag flew over Spain's colonial empire in the New World, including St. Augustine.

The Florida State Flag. Do you see a similarity between the Burgundy Flag and the Florida State Flag? Note that the Florida flag honors both the Spanish and the Native Americans (though the Indian shown is a Seminole, who arrived later in Florida).

St. Augustine was founded in 1565, which was 55 years before the Pilgrims landed in Massachusetts in 1620. St. Augustine has remained a permanent settlement since the day the Spanish and the Timucua celebrated with their feast of thanksgiving. Battles have been fought, and city governments have come and gone, but St. Augustine has endured. As the importance of St. Augustine continues to be uncovered, we now know it's not only the oldest city in the United States, but the site of America's first Thanksgiving as well.

*Menéndez parade celebrating
St. Augustine's founder.*

*Annual Menéndez Birthday Gala.
A period costume event is held every
year to celebrate the birthday
of Menéndez on the last Saturday
in February.*

Why, you may ask, don't the history books record that the first Thanksgiving was in St. Augustine, Florida? Well, for many reasons England grew to be the dominant culture in the United States, and it is from their viewpoint that much of our history is told. But as time passes and unknown facts come to light, a more detailed history emerges from our heritage. And every year, more and more people join in celebrating our country's first Thanksgiving by serving *cocido* as the honored meal of the day.

Most early cooking in St. Augustine was in a stew pot over a fire. The Timucua taught the Spanish to roast meat on spits and smoke fish on a wooden grill. Early St. Augustine ovens for baking bread were made of coquina, a material composed mostly of bits of seashells, which was also used to build the *castillo* in St. Augustine.

The famous Spanish chorizo sausage is used in this modern version of *cocido,* which is a type of *sopa de garbanzo* (garbanzo bean soup.) Note that garbanzos are also called chickpeas.

Cocido Recipe

16-20 ounces garbanzos (chickpeas)
8 cups water
1 teaspoon pepper
1 teaspoon saffron
1 large clove garlic, minced
1 leek, cut into short lengths

½ pound sausage, sliced (fresh chorizo if preferred) *
½ pound salt pork**, diced
1 medium onion, diced
2 medium potatoes, diced
½ head green cabbage, quartered
2 large carrots, thickly sliced

Drain beans, rinse, and put in large kettle. Add water, spices, and garlic. In skillet, fry salt pork and onions until brown. Drain, then add to kettle. Simmer for 2 hours. Add remaining ingredients and simmer 45 minutes.

* Regular sausage works nicely. Chorizo has a distinct flavor.

**Bacon, ham, or pancetta may be substituted for salt pork.

(For other historic Spanish recipes, see Maggi Smith Hall, *Flavors of St. Augustine: An Historic Cookbook)*

Timeline

1492	Christopher Columbus, funded by the Spanish crown, lands in the New World at an island in the Bahamas.
1513	Spaniard Juan Ponce de León is the first European to land in Florida, somewhere along the northeast coast.
1539	Spaniard Hernando de Soto lands on the west coast of Florida.
1564	Establishment of Fort Caroline at the mouth of the St. Johns River (north of St. Augustine) by the French.
1565	July. Sent by King Philip II of Spain, Pedro Menéndez sails from Spain to confront the French in Florida.
	August 28. Pedro Menéndez arrives off the coast of Florida.
	September 7. Father Francisco López de Mendoza Grajales goes ashore to prepare for Menéndez's arrival on land.
	September 8. Menéndez comes ashore at the Timucua village of Seloy, naming the site St. Augustine. A special Mass of Thanksgiving is given and the first thanksgiving feast takes place.
1598	A thanksgiving ceremony and feast are held near what is now El Paso, Texas, by Spaniard Juan de Oñate and natives of the region.
1607	First permanent English settlement in North America is established at Jamestown, Virginia.
1620	English colonists, the Pilgrims, land in Plymouth, Massachusetts.
1621	The Pilgrims have a feast with the native peoples in the fall after their first harvest.

Glossary

A.D.
Used to show dates taking place after the birth of Christ. It stands for the Latin *Anno Domini,* which means "Year of the Lord."

admiral
A naval officer of the highest rank, the commander in chief of the fleet.

archaeology
The study of historic cultures by digging up artifacts and other remains.

artillery
Large weapons such as cannons.

chaplain
A member of the clergy, in this case connected to the royal court.

chiefdom
The territory or people over which a chief rules.

cocido
A rich Spanish stew.

Franciscans
Members of a religious order serving as missionaries. Part of the Franciscan faith was to live in poverty and humility.

Gulf Stream
An ocean current that runs from the Gulf of Mexico, through the Straits of Florida, and along the eastern coast of the United States.

imposing
Very impressive in appearance or ability.

inlet
An indentation of a shoreline, usually long and narrow. An arm of a larger body of water.

Jesuit
A member of a Roman Catholic religious order, the Society of Jesus.

loincloth
A piece of clothing worn to cover the area around the hips.

missionaries
A group sent on a religious mission to a foreign country.

notary
A person who is legally able to witness signatures and documents.

provisions
Needed supplies, usually food.

Renaissance
A period in European history between the 14th and 17th centuries when the Middle Ages were coming to an end and the modern world was beginning to rise. There was a rebirth of interest in learning, art, and exploration.

sea-lanes
Regularly used ocean routes followed by ships.

Spanish Inquisition
An institution used by the Spanish government to control society from the 15th to the 17th century.

Timucua
A Native American people formerly inhabiting much of northern Florida. They became extinct in the early 18th century.

thatch
A tightly bound layer of dead plants (in Florida, palm leaves) used to cover a roof.

treasure fleet
From the 16th to the 18th century a convoy (group) of Spanish ships that transported European goods to the Spanish colonies in the Americas and brought back products such as gold and silver.

weir
A barrier set in a stream for catching fish.

References

Articles

Bennet, Charles E. "Maytime," in *Laudonnière and Fort Caroline: History and Documents.* Tuscaloosa, AL: University of Alabama Press, 2001, pp. 65–70.

Gannon, Michael. "The Real First Thanksgiving Meal," *Forum*, Fall 2006, pp. 10–11.

Gannon, Michael. "We Gather Together . . .," *St. Augustine Catholic*, October/November 2002, pp. 8–9.

López de Mendoza Grajales, Francisco. "The Founding of St. Augustine, 1565." *Modern History Sourcebook*: www.fordham.edu/halsall/mod/1565staugustine.html. From: Oliver J. Thatcher, ed., *The Library of Original Sources* (Milwaukee: University Research Extension Co., 1907), Vol. V: 9th to 16th Centuries, pp. 327–341.

"St. Augustine, America's Oldest City," *Cobblestone*, November 1995, Volume 16, Number 9. (Entire issue is on St. Augustine.)

Books

Bushnell, Amy. *The King's Coffer: Proprietors of the Spanish Royal Treasury, 1565–1702.* Gainesville, FL: University Press of Florida, 1981.

Hall, Maggi Smith. *Flavors of St. Augustine: An Historic Cookbook.* Lake Buena Vista, FL: Tailored Tours Publications, 1999.

Lyon, Eugene. *Richer Than We Thought: The Material Culture of Sixteenth Century St. Augustine.* Vol. 29 of *El Escribano.* St Augustine, FL: St. Augustine Historical Society, 1992.

Matthews, Rupert. Explorer (DK Eyewitness Books). New York: DK Publishing, 2005.

Narrative of Le Moyne, an Artist Who Accompanied the French Expedition to Florida under Laudonnière, 1564. Boston: Tames R. Osgood and Company (Late Ticknor and Fields, and Fields, Osgood & Co.), 1875. Republished by the University of Florida Libraries, Gainesville, FL, 2005.

Old European Cities, Thirty-Two 16th-Century City Maps and Text from the Civitates Orbis Terrarum of Georg Braun & Franz Hogenberg with a Description by Ruthhardt Oehme of Early Map-Making Techniques. London: Thames and Hudson, 1965.

Waterbury, Jean Parker, editor. *The Oldest City.* St Augustine, FL: St. Augustine Historical Society, 1983. (Authors: Dr. George E. Buker, Dr. Amy Bushnell, Robert N. Dow, Jr., Dr. Thomas Graham, John W. Griffin, Patricia C. Griffin, Dr. Daniel Shafer, Jean Parker Waterbury)

Weitzel, Kelley. *The Timucua: A Native American Detective Story.* Gainesville, FL: University Press of Florida, 2000.

Wickham, Joan Adams. *Food Favorites of St. Augustine.* St. Augustine, FL: C. F. Hamblen, 1973.

Websites

Florida Humanities Council
  www.flahum.org/colonial
Publication of Archival Library and Museum Materials
  http://palmm.fcla.edu/map/mapfl.shtml
Dioceses of St. Augustine
  http://www.dosafl.com/index.php?page=history/historical_overview

Acknowledgments

The National Endowment for the Humanities is to be commended for funding the workshop *Between Columbus and Jamestown: Spanish St. Augustine,* held in 2005. Without this workshop, parts of our national heritage would go unnoticed. Monica Rowland and the NEH workshop presenters shone in both their knowledge of the subject and the passion they hold. I thank Dr. Michael Gannon for his extensive research in Florida history. If not for his connecting of the dots, the fact that St. Augustine is the site of the first Thanksgiving may have remained hidden. I am grateful to Senior Preserve Naturalist Kelley Weitzel of the Pelotes (Timucua) Nature Preserve for the sharing of her resources and intimate understanding of the Timucua people. A special thanks to Jim Cusick, from the University of Florida, Department of Special and Area Studies Collections, George A. Smathers Libraries, for reviewing the manuscript and making suggestions for historical accuracy.

Without the expertise and guidance of Charles Tingley of the St. Augustine Historical Society, this book would not have been possible. In truth, his knowledge on the subject is so vast that only a small portion comes to light in these pages. And I appreciate the willingness of Dr. John McGrath, from Boston University, to read the manuscript in its final stage. Of course, in spite of all the help I've had from these experts, any errors that may have crept in are my own.

Author's Note

I was in St. Augustine, Florida, attending a weeklong Florida Humanities Council teacher workshop (funded by the National Endowment for the Humanities) titled *Between Columbus and Jamestown: Spanish St. Augustine* when I heard that St. Augustine was the site of America's first Thanksgiving. I knew St. Augustine was the oldest city in the United States but nothing more. I was intrigued. As I experienced the streets and architecture of historic St. Augustine, listened to lectures by distinguished professionals and University of Florida professors, read firsthand historical accounts, witnessed an archaeological dig, and toured the fort called Castillo de San Marcos, I learned it was indeed true. Evidence did indicate the first American Thanksgiving took place in St. Augustine on the eighth of September in 1565. And interestingly enough, it involved Europeans settling in a new land, Native Americans, religious belief, and a feast.

Dr. Michael Gannon, professor emeritus of history at the University of Florida, is known for his extensive research on the state of Florida. He was given the nickname "the Grinch who stole Thanksgiving" by some New Englanders when he revealed his St. Augustine findings. Dr. Gannon states in his 1965 book entitled *The Cross in the Sand,* "It was the first community act of religion and thanksgiving in the first permanent [European] settlement in the land." He explains: "The keyword in that sentence was 'permanent.' Numerous thanksgivings for a safe voyage and landing had been made before in Florida by Ponce de Leon (and others). . . . But all of those ventures, Catholic and Calvinist, failed to put down permanent roots. St. Augustine's ceremonies were important historically in that they took place in what would develop into a permanently occupied European city, North America's first. . . . The thanksgiving at St. Augustine, celebrated 56 years before the Puritan-Pilgrim thanksgiving at Plymouth Plantation (Massachusetts), did not, however, become the origin of a national annual tradition, as Plymouth would. The reason is that, as the maxim holds, it is the victors who write the histories."

Dr. Gannon, with a chuckle in his voice, summed it up this way: "In the year 1621, when the Pilgrims were having their first Thanksgiving, St. Augustine was up for urban renewal."

Index

CPSIA information can be obtained at www.ICGtesting.com
Printed in the USA
LVOW01s1042030914

402187LV00001B/1/P

31901055850921

9 781561 647125